T0163117

EMOJIS
The Starter Book

New Number and Logic Puzzles

How it all began

In May 2000 I had an accident, falling from a ladder, and needed 5 months off work.

Boredom soon set in and as I love numbers I decided to try and devise some number puzzles.

I put three rows of numbers from 1 to 9 on a spreadsheet. I then inserted a formula that added the middle number to the top and bottom numbers and printed out the result.

I then erased all the numbers just leaving the top and bottom totals then by using addition tried to reinstate the correct numbers.

It was then that I had that "Eureka" moment, realising that because the middle row was common to both sums, up and down, it would need logic to place the correct combinations in the right order, and so my ZYGO puzzle was born!

I had a new addictive hobby.

In the years that followed I devised many new number puzzles and compiled computer programs that generated them automatically.

A year or two ago, I thought I would try and get some puzzles published and contacted Andrew Griffin at Tarquin who decided to publish 6 puzzle books for everyone to enjoy.

EMOJIS

The Starter Book

Easier New Number and Logic Puzzles

Les Page

Tarquin

Publisher's Note

If you have enjoyed this Emojis book and want a further challenge there is a tougher version of Emojis. This and 4 other books are described below - fuller details on www.tarquingroup.com. Enjoy!

Samples of some of the puzzles in other books can be found at the back of this book.

Les Page has asserted his right to be identified as the author of this work under the Copyright, Designs and Patents Act 1988.

All rights reserved. No part of this publication may be reproduced, stored any means in a retrieval system, or transmitted in any form or by any means, electronic, mechanical, photocopying, recording or otherwise without the prior permission of the copyright owner.

© Les Page 2020

ISBN UK (Book) 978-1-913565-08-4

ISBN (EBook) 978-1-913565-09-1

Designed and Printed in the UK

Tarquin

Suite 74, 17 Holywell Hill

St Albans AL1 1DT

UK

www.tarquingroup.com

Emojis The Starter Book
Contents

Puzzles 1–24

Start on page 1 overleaf. Solutions to each are on reverse side of the puzzle page.

Bonus Puzzles

On page 49–60 there are some bonus puzzles from other books in the series. These books are set out below. If you enjoy a particular puzzle from the bonuses, get the whole book from your usual bookseller or from www.tarquingroup.com

Emojis - tougher puzzles
Book ISBN 9781913565008
Ebook ISBN 9781913565015

Emojis - tougher puzzles
Book ISBN 9781913565008
Ebook ISBN 9781913565015

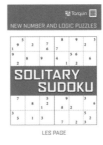

Emojis - tougher puzzles
Book ISBN 9781913565008
Ebook ISBN 9781913565015

The Compendium
Book ISBN 9781913565060
Ebook ISBN 9781913565077

Nightmare Blocks - The Starter Book
Book ISBN 9781913565107
Ebook ISBN 9781913565114

PUZZLE 1

15 EMOJIS have different numerical values. Put the values in the puzzle grid to agree the sum totals horizontally, vertically and diagonally.

Cross out numerical values when placed

↓ = ∩ Enter values when worked out   Yellow boxes are "given" values

1 x	👆	=	
2 x	😐	=	
1 x	👉	=	
2 x	✦	=	
2 x	✈	=	
2 x	✋	=	19
2 x	☹	=	7
2 x	☺	=	
1 x	👍	=	
2 x	💣	=	10
2 x	⌘	=	16
1 x	☝	=	
2 x	🏳	=	2
1 x	👎	=	21
2 x	☠	=	

↘	↓	↓	↓	↓	↓	↙
→	😐	👎	⌘	✋	✈	67
→	✈	⌘	☺	🏳	☠	47
→	👆	✦	✋	😐	☠	68
→	☝	☹	🏳	💣	✦	36
→	👍	☹	☺	💣	👉	38
41	40	62	45	44	65	60

↘	↓	↓	↓	↓	↓	↙
→		21	16	19		67
→		16		2		47
→			19			68
→		7	2	10		36
→		7		10		38
41	40	62	45	44	65	60

2
3
4
5
6
7
8
10
11
12
16
17
18
19
21

Solution Overleaf

© Les Page 2020   ISBN 9781913565084

For more www.tarquingroup.com

SOLUTION 1

↘	↓	↓	↓	↓	↓	↙
→	😐	👎	⌘	🖐	✈	67
→	✈	⌘	☺	🏳	☠	47
→	👉	❖	🖐	😐	☠	68
→	☝	☹	🏳	💣	❖	36
→	👍	☹	☺	💣	👉	38
41	40	62	45	44	65	60

↘	↓	↓	↓	↓	↓	↙
→	3	21	16	19	8	67
→	8	16	4	2	17	47
→	18	11	19	3	17	68
→	6	7	2	10	11	36
→	5	7	4	10	12	38
41	40	62	45	44	65	60

Emoji		Value
🏳	=	2
😐	=	3
☺	=	4
👍	=	5
☝	=	6
☹	=	7
✈	=	8
💣	=	10
❖	=	11
👉	=	12
⌘	=	16
☠	=	17
👉	=	18
🖐	=	19
👎	=	21

© Les Page 2020   ISBN 9781913565084

For more www.tarquingroup.com

PUZZLE 2

15 EMOJIS have different numerical values. Put the values in the puzzle grid to agree the sum totals horizontally, vertically and diagonally.

Cross out numerical values when placed

↓ = ↻ Enter values when worked out   Yellow boxes are "given" values

1 x	☜	=	
2 x	😐	=	4
1 x	☞	=	
2 x	❖	=	
2 x	✈	=	
2 x	🖐	=	6
2 x	☹	=	3
2 x	☺	=	
1 x	👍	=	
2 x	💣	=	8
2 x	⌘	=	
1 x	☝	=	
2 x	🏴	=	15
1 x	👎	=	
2 x	☠	=	14

↘	↓	↓	↓	↓	↓	↙
→	🏴	⌘	⌘	☜	👍	66
→	🖐	💣	❖	🖐	✈	55
→	☹	☺	☹	👎	☝	51
→	☠	☠	☞	😐	💣	52
→	✈	🏴	😐	❖	☺	72
59	54	68	51	44	79	48

↘	↓	↓	↓	↓	↓	↙
→	15					66
→	6	8		6		55
→	3		3			51
→	14	14		4	8	52
→		15	4			72
59	54	68	51	44	79	48

Right-hand value list: 3, 4, 5, 6, 8, 10, 12, 13, 14, 15, 16, 17, 18, 19, 20

Solution Overleaf

© Les Page 2020   ISBN 9781913565084   For more www.tarquingroup.com

SOLUTION 2

↘	↓	↓	↓	↓	↓	↙
→	🏳	⌘	⌘	☞	👍	66
→	✋	💣	❖	🖐	✈	55
→	☹	☺	☹	👎	☝	51
→	☠	☠	☞	☺	💣	52
→	✈	🏳	☺	❖	☺	72
59	54	68	51	44	79	48

☹	=	3
☺	=	4
☞	=	5
✋	=	6
💣	=	8
👎	=	10
☞	=	12
⌘	=	13
☠	=	14
🏳	=	15
✈	=	16
☝	=	17
☺	=	18
❖	=	19
👍	=	20

↘	↓	↓	↓	↓	↓	↙
→	15	13	13	5	20	66
→	6	8	19	6	16	55
→	3	18	3	10	17	51
→	14	14	12	4	8	52
→	16	15	4	19	18	72
59	54	68	51	44	79	48

© Les Page 2020   ISBN 9781913565084

EMOJIS CHAIN REACTION

PUZZLE 3

15 EMOJIS have different numerical values. Put the values in the puzzle grid to agree the sum totals horizontally, vertically and diagonally.

Cross out numerical values when placed

	↓	=	⋂	Enter values when worked out	Yellow boxes are "given" values

1 x	🐦	=	9
2 x	😐	=	20
1 x	👉	=	
2 x	❖	=	
2 x	✈	=	
2 x	🖐	=	12
2 x	☹	=	
2 x	☺	=	16
1 x	👍	=	
2 x	💣	=	
2 x	⌘	=	14
1 x	☝	=	
2 x	🏳	=	
1 x	👇	=	5
2 x	☠	=	

↘	↓	↓	↓	↓	↓	↙
→	💣	🖐	😐	☹	☺	70
→	☠	⌘	☠	👍	🏳	28
→	☹	💣	☺	👍	🖐	57
→	🏳	😐	✈	🐦	⌘	59
→	❖	✈	☝	👉	❖	81
78	48	80	68	35	64	79

↘	↓	↓	↓	↓	↓	↙
→		12	20		16	70
→		14		5		28
→			16		12	57
→		20		9	14	59
→						81
78	48	80	68	35	64	79

1
3
4
5
7
9
11
12
13
14
15
16
19
20
21

Solution Overleaf

© Les Page 2020   ISBN 9781913565084
For more www.tarquingroup.com

EMOJIS CHAIN REACTION

LEVEL E

SOLUTION 3

↘	↓	↓	↓	↓	↓	↙
→	💣	🖐	😐	☹	☺	70
→	☠	⌘	☠	👎	🏳	28
→	☹	💣	☺	👍	🖐	57
→	🏳	😐	✈	👉	⌘	59
→	❖	✈	☝	☞	❖	81
78	48	80	68	35	64	79

🏳	=	1
☹	=	3
☠	=	4
👎	=	5
👍	=	7
👉	=	9
☞	=	11
🖐	=	12
☝	=	13
⌘	=	14
✈	=	15
☺	=	16
💣	=	19
😐	=	20
❖	=	21

↘	↓	↓	↓	↓	↓	↙
→	19	12	20	3	16	70
→	4	14	4	5	1	28
→	3	19	16	7	12	57
→	1	20	15	9	14	59
→	21	15	13	11	21	81
78	48	80	68	35	64	79

© Les Page 2020   ISBN 9781913565084

For more www.tarquingroup.com

EMOJIS CHAIN REACTION

Cross out numerical values when placed

PUZZLE 4

15 EMOJIS have different numerical values. Put the values in the puzzle grid to agree the sum totals horizontally, vertically and diagonally.

↓ = ⤵ Enter values when worked out   Yellow boxes are "given" values

1 x	👆	=	
2 x	😐	=	
1 x	👉	=	
2 x	❖	=	20
2 x	✈	=	3
2 x	🖐	=	
2 x	☹	=	19
2 x	😊	=	
1 x	👍	=	5
2 x	💣	=	
2 x	⌘	=	
1 x	☝	=	
2 x	🏳	=	7
1 x	👎	=	4
2 x	☠	=	8

↘	↓	↓	↓	↓	↓	↙
→	👆	💣	👎	🖐	🖐	44
→	😊	❖	☠	☠	❖	67
→	😊	👉	✈	😐	⌘	47
→	😐	☹	⌘	🏳	☹	65
→	👍	💣	☝	✈	🏳	37
37	48	94	30	26	62	52

↘	↓	↓	↓	↓	↓	↙
→			4			44
→		20	8	8	20	67
→			3			47
→		19		7	19	65
→	5			3	7	37
37	48	94	30	26	62	52

1	2	3	4	5	6	7	8	11	13	14	15	19	20	21

Solution Overleaf

© Les Page 2020   ISBN 9781913565084   For more www.tarquingroup.com

EMOJIS CHAIN REACTION

LEVEL E

SOLUTION 4

↘	↓	↓	↓	↓	↓	↙
→	👉	💣	👎	✋	✋	44
→	☺	❖	☠	☠	❖	67
→	☺	👉	✈	😐	⌘	47
→	😐	☹	⌘	🏳	☹	65
→	👍	💣	☝	✈	🏳	37
37	48	94	30	26	62	52

☝	=	1
✋	=	2
✈	=	3
👎	=	4
👍	=	5
😐	=	6
🏳	=	7
☠	=	8
☺	=	11
👉	=	13
⌘	=	14
👉	=	15
☹	=	19
❖	=	20
💣	=	21

↘	↓	↓	↓	↓	↓	↙
→	15	21	4	2	2	44
→	11	20	8	8	20	67
→	11	13	3	6	14	47
→	6	19	14	7	19	65
→	5	21	1	3	7	37
37	48	94	30	26	62	52

© Les Page 2020   ISBN 9781913565084

EMOJIS CHAIN REACTION

LEVEL **E**

PUZZLE 5

15 EMOJIS have different numerical values. Put the values in the puzzle grid to agree the sum totals horizontally, vertically and diagonally.

Cross out numerical values when placed

↓ = ↺ Enter values when worked out   Yellow boxes are "given" values

		=	
1 x	👉	=	
2 x	😐	=	
1 x	👉	=	
2 x	◆	=	
2 x	✈	=	3
2 x	✋	=	6
2 x	☹	=	
2 x	☺	=	8
1 x	👍	=	
2 x	💣	=	
2 x	⌘	=	
1 x	☝	=	2
2 x	🏳	=	
1 x	👉	=	16
2 x	☠	=	18

Top grid

↘	↓	↓	↓	↓	↓	↙
→	✈	💣	🏳	◆	☹	70
→	◆	☠	👉	☺	✋	63
→	👉	😐	👍	☹	☠	60
→	✈	✋	☺	☝	😐	23
→	💣	👍	⌘	🏳	⌘	81
58	62	66	66	56	47	51

Bottom grid

↘	↓	↓	↓	↓	↓	↙
→	3					70
→		18		8	6	63
→			16		18	60
→	3	6	8	2		23
→						81
58	62	66	66	56	47	51

Cross out numerical values

✗
2
3
4
6
7
8
11
12
15
16
17
18
19
20
21

Solution Overleaf

© Les Page 2020   ISBN 9781913565084   For more www.tarquingroup.com

EMOJIS
CHAIN REACTION

LEVEL **E**

SOLUTION 5

↘	↓	↓	↓	↓	↓	↙
→	✈	💣	🏳	❖	☹	70
→	❖	☠	👉	☺	🖐	63
→	👉	😐	👎	☹	☠	60
→	✈	🖐	☺	☝	😐	23
→	💣	👍	⌘	🏳	⌘	81
58	62	66	66	56	47	51

↘	↓	↓	↓	↓	↓	↙
→	3	21	19	20	7	70
→	20	18	11	8	6	63
→	15	4	16	7	18	60
→	3	6	8	2	4	23
→	21	17	12	19	12	81
58	62	66	66	56	47	51

☝	=	2
✈	=	3
😐	=	4
🖐	=	6
☹	=	7
☺	=	8
👉	=	11
⌘	=	12
👉	=	15
👎	=	16
👍	=	17
☠	=	18
🏳	=	19
❖	=	20
💣	=	21

© Les Page 2020   ISBN 9781913565084

For more www.tarquingroup.com

EMOJIS CHAIN REACTION

LEVEL E

PUZZLE 6

15 EMOJIS have different numerical values. Put the values in the puzzle grid to agree the sum totals horizontally, vertically and diagonally.

↓ = ↻ Enter values when worked out   Yellow boxes are "given" values

Cross out numerical values when placed

Qty	Emoji	=	Value
1 x	🤙	=	
2 x	😐	=	
1 x	👉	=	
2 x	❖	=	15
2 x	✈	=	
2 x	✋	=	10
2 x	☹	=	2
2 x	☺	=	5
1 x	👍	=	
2 x	💣	=	
2 x	⌘	=	
1 x	☝	=	21
2 x	🏁	=	
1 x	👇	=	4
2 x	☠	=	

↘	↓	↓	↓	↓	↓	↙
→	☹	😐	💣	👎	☠	47
→	✈	✋	❖	☹	⌘	56
→	☺	👍	☺	👉	💣	43
→	✈	☝	✋	❖	☠	70
→	🏁	😐	🏁	👉	⌘	79
55	61	77	68	33	56	44

↘	↓	↓	↓	↓	↓	↙
→	2			4		47
→		10	15	2		56
→	5		5			43
→		21	10	15		70
→						79
55	61	77	68	33	56	44

Values
1
2
4
5
7
10
11
12
14
15
16
17
18
20
21

Solution Overleaf

© Les Page 2020   ISBN 9781913565084   For more www.tarquingroup.com

SOLUTION 6

↘	↓	↓	↓	↓	↓	↙
→	😞	😐	💣	👎	☠	47
→	✈	✋	❖	😞	⌘	56
→	☺	👍	☺	👉	💣	43
→	✈	☝	✋	❖	☠	70
→	🏳	😐	🏳	👉	⌘	79
55	61	77	68	33	56	44

↘	↓	↓	↓	↓	↓	↙
→	2	16	18	4	7	47
→	17	10	15	2	12	56
→	5	14	5	1	18	43
→	17	21	10	15	7	70
→	20	16	20	11	12	79
55	61	77	68	33	56	44

👉	=	1
😞	=	2
👎	=	4
☺	=	5
☠	=	7
✋	=	10
👉	=	11
⌘	=	12
👍	=	14
❖	=	15
😐	=	16
✈	=	17
💣	=	18
🏳	=	20
☝	=	21

© Les Page 2020   ISBN 9781913565084

EMOJIS CHAIN REACTION

 LEVEL E

PUZZLE 7

15 EMOJIS have different numerical values. Put the values in the puzzle grid to agree the sum totals horizontally, vertically and diagonally.

 Cross out numerical values when placed

↓ = ↩ Enter values when worked out   Yellow boxes are "given" values

		=	
1 x	👉	=	
2 x	😐	=	
1 x	👉	=	16
2 x	❖	=	
2 x	✈	=	13
2 x	✋	=	
2 x	☹	=	21
2 x	☺	=	6
1 x	👍	=	
2 x	💣	=	20
2 x	⌘	=	18
1 x	☝	=	
2 x	🏴	=	
1 x	👎	=	
2 x	☠	=	

↘	↓	↓	↓	↓	↓	↙
→	😊	😊	👉	✈	❖	48
→	🏴	✈	🏴	☹	☠	67
→	👎	✋	👉	☹	👍	57
→	😐	⌘	⌘	💣	☠	85
→	😐	💣	✋	☝	❖	49
76	41	64	63	76	62	64

↘	↓	↓	↓	↓	↓	↙
→	6	6		13		48
→		13		21		67
→			16	21		57
→		18	18	20		85
→		20				49
76	41	64	63	76	62	64

1
3
6
7
8
9
10
12
13
14
16
17
18
20
21

Solution Overleaf

© Les Page 2020   ISBN 9781913565084   For more www.tarquingroup.com

EMOJIS
CHAIN REACTION

SOLUTION 7

↘	↓	↓	↓	↓	↓	↙
→	☺	☺	👉	✈	✤	48
→	🚩	✈	🚩	☹	☠	67
→	👎	🖐	👉	☹	👍	57
→	😐	⌘	⌘	💣	☠	85
→	😐	💣	🖐	☝	✤	49
76	41	64	63	76	62	64

↘	↓	↓	↓	↓	↓	↙
→	6	6	14	13	9	48
→	8	13	8	21	17	67
→	3	7	16	21	10	57
→	12	18	18	20	17	85
→	12	20	7	1	9	49
76	41	64	63	76	62	64

Symbol		Value
☝	=	1
👎	=	3
☺	=	6
🖐	=	7
🚩	=	8
✤	=	9
👍	=	10
😐	=	12
✈	=	13
👉	=	14
👉	=	16
☠	=	17
⌘	=	18
💣	=	20
☹	=	21

© Les Page 2020 ISBN 9781913565084   For more www.tarquingroup.com

EMOJIS CHAIN REACTION

PUZZLE 8

15 EMOJIS have different numerical values. Put the values in the puzzle grid to agree the sum totals horizontally, vertically and diagonally.

Cross out numerical values when placed

↓		=	↻	Enter values when worked out

Yellow boxes are "given" values

1 x	👉	=	17
2 x	😐	=	
1 x	👉	=	18
2 x	❖	=	
2 x	✈	=	2
2 x	🖐	=	
2 x	☹	=	
2 x	☺	=	1
1 x	👍	=	3
2 x	💣	=	20
2 x	⌘	=	
1 x	☝	=	
2 x	🏳	=	
1 x	👎	=	5
2 x	☠	=	

↘	↓	↓	↓	↓	↓	↙
→	🏳	🖐	⌘	😐	👉	77
→	🖐	👍	☹	☺	⌘	39
→	☠	☺	👎	👉	🏳	52
→	❖	💣	☠	✈	❖	63
→	☹	😐	✈	☝	💣	56
49	69	61	34	49	74	45

↘	↓	↓	↓	↓	↓	↙
→					17	77
→	3			1		39
→		1	5	18		52
→		20		2		63
→			2		20	56
49	69	61	34	49	74	45

✗	
	1
	2
	3
	5
	6
	8
	12
	13
	14
	15
	16
	17
	18
	20
	21

Solution Overleaf

© Les Page 2020   ISBN 9781913565084

For more www.tarquingroup.com

EMOJIS
CHAIN REACTION

LEVEL **E**

SOLUTION 8

↘	↓	↓	↓	↓	↓	↙
→	🏳	✋	⌘	😐	👇	77
→	✋	👍	☹	☺	⌘	39
→	☠	☺	👎	👉	🏳	52
→	❖	💣	☠	✈	❖	63
→	☹	😐	✈	☝	💣	56
49	69	61	34	49	74	45

☺	=	1
✈	=	2
👍	=	3
👎	=	5
☹	=	6
⌘	=	8
☝	=	12
☠	=	13
❖	=	14
🏳	=	15
😐	=	16
👇	=	17
👉	=	18
💣	=	20
✋	=	21

↘	↓	↓	↓	↓	↓	↙
→	15	21	8	16	17	77
→	21	3	6	1	8	39
→	13	1	5	18	15	52
→	14	20	13	2	14	63
→	6	16	2	12	20	56
49	69	61	34	49	74	45

© Les Page 2020   ISBN 9781913565084

EMOJIS CHAIN REACTION

LEVEL **E**

PUZZLE 9

15 EMOJIS have different numerical values. Put the values in the puzzle grid to agree the sum totals horizontally, vertically and diagonally.

Cross out numerical values when placed

↓ = ↺ Enter values when worked out   Yellow boxes are "given" values

1 x	👉	=	5
2 x	😐	=	19
1 x	👉	=	
2 x	❖	=	17
2 x	✈	=	
2 x	🖐	=	
2 x	😦	=	
2 x	😊	=	
1 x	👍	=	6
2 x	💣	=	
2 x	⌘	=	
1 x	☝	=	3
2 x	🏳	=	20
1 x	👎	=	
2 x	☠	=	

↘	↓	↓	↓	↓	↓	↙
→	😦	☠	👍	🏳	✈	70
→	☠	👉	👎	😐	😊	44
→	⌘	😦	☝	✈	👉	61
→	🖐	🏳	💣	❖	😊	63
→	❖	🖐	💣	⌘	😐	70
73	71	64	30	85	58	62

↘	↓	↓	↓	↓	↓	↙
→			6	20		70
→		5		19		44
→			3			61
→		20		17		63
→	17				19	70
73	71	64	30	85	58	62

1
3
5
6
7
9
10
11
12
14
15
17
18
19
20

Solution Overleaf

© Les Page 2020   ISBN 9781913565084   For more www.tarquingroup.com

EMOJIS
CHAIN REACTION

LEVEL **E**

SOLUTION 9

↘	↓	↓	↓	↓	↓	↙
→	☹	☠	👍	🚩	✈	70
→	☠	👉	👎	😐	☺	44
→	⌘	☹	☝	✈	👉	61
→	🖐	🚩	💣	❖	☺	63
→	❖	🖐	💣	⌘	😐	70
73	71	64	30	85	58	62

↘	↓	↓	↓	↓	↓	↙
→	18	12	6	20	14	70
→	12	5	1	19	7	44
→	15	18	3	14	11	61
→	9	20	10	17	7	63
→	17	9	10	15	19	70
73	71	64	30	85	58	62

👎	=	1
☝	=	3
👉	=	5
👍	=	6
☺	=	7
🖐	=	9
💣	=	10
👉	=	11
☠	=	12
✈	=	14
⌘	=	15
❖	=	17
☹	=	18
😐	=	19
🚩	=	20

© Les Page 2020   ISBN 9781913565084

For more www.tarquingroup.com

EMOJIS CHAIN REACTION

LEVEL E

PUZZLE 10

15 EMOJIS have different numerical values. Put the values in the puzzle grid to agree the sum totals horizontally, vertically and diagonally.

Cross out numerical values when placed

↓ = ∩ Enter values when worked out   Yellow boxes are "given" values

1 x	👆	=	
2 x	😐	=	7
1 x	👉	=	
2 x	❖	=	15
2 x	✈	=	3
2 x	🖐	=	17
2 x	☹	=	
2 x	☺	=	
1 x	👍	=	
2 x	💣	=	
2 x	⌘	=	
1 x	☝	=	20
2 x	🚩	=	
1 x	👎	=	4
2 x	☠	=	18

↘	↓	↓	↓	↓	↓	↙
→	⌘	🖐	😐	❖	🚩	72
→	👉	✈	👍	☠	☺	43
→	☺	☠	😐	✈	☝	56
→	☹	❖	👉	🖐	🚩	63
→	☹	⌘	💣	💣	👎	46
55	34	72	50	64	60	50

↘	↓	↓	↓	↓	↓	↙
→		17	7	15		72
→		3		18		43
→		18	7	3	20	56
→		15		17		63
→					4	46
55	34	72	50	64	60	50

| 1 |
| 3 |
| 4 |
| 5 |
| 7 |
| 8 |
| 9 |
| 11 |
| 14 |
| 15 |
| 16 |
| 17 |
| 18 |
| 19 |
| 20 |

Solution Overleaf

© Les Page 2020   ISBN 9781913565084   For more www.tarquingroup.com

EMOJIS CHAIN REACTION

SOLUTION 10

↘	↓	↓	↓	↓	↓	↙
→	⌘	🖐	😐	✜	🏳	72
→	👈	✈	👍	☠	😊	43
→	😊	☠	😐	✈	☝	56
→	☹	✜	👉	🖐	🏳	63
→	☹	⌘	💣	💣	👎	46
55	34	72	50	64	60	50

☹	=	1
✈	=	3
👎	=	4
👈	=	5
😐	=	7
😊	=	8
👍	=	9
💣	=	11
🏳	=	14
✜	=	15
👉	=	16
🖐	=	17
☠	=	18
⌘	=	19
☝	=	20

↘	↓	↓	↓	↓	↓	↙
→	19	17	7	15	14	72
→	5	3	9	18	8	43
→	8	18	7	3	20	56
→	1	15	16	17	14	63
→	1	19	11	11	4	46
55	34	72	50	64	60	50

© Les Page 2020   ISBN 9781913565084

EMOJIS CHAIN REACTION

PUZZLE 11

15 EMOJIS have different numerical values. Put the values in the puzzle grid to agree the sum totals horizontally, vertically and diagonally.

Cross out numerical values when placed

↓ = ∩ Enter values when worked out   Yellow boxes are "given" values

1 x	👆	=	14
2 x	😐	=	
1 x	👉	=	
2 x	❖	=	
2 x	✈	=	5
2 x	🖐	=	
2 x	☹	=	19
2 x	☺	=	21
1 x	👍	=	
2 x	💣	=	3
2 x	⌘	=	
1 x	☝	=	
2 x	🏳	=	
1 x	👎	=	4
2 x	☠	=	10

↘	↓	↓	↓	↓	↓	↙
→	👍	☝	😐	✈	☠	46
→	😐	☹	🖐	👆	❖	49
→	👎	🏳	💣	🖐	☠	32
→	🏳	✈	⌘	☺	💣	45
→	⌘	☹	☺	❖	👉	68
39	33	70	39	54	44	67

↘	↓	↓	↓	↓	↓	↙
→				5	10	46
→		19		14		49
→	4		3		10	32
→		5		21	3	45
→		19	21			68
39	33	70	39	54	44	67

Values
2
3
4
5
6
7
8
9
10
11
13
14
18
19
21

Solution Overleaf

© Les Page 2020   ISBN 9781913565084

For more www.tarquingroup.com

SOLUTION 11

↘	↓	↓	↓	↓	↓	↙
→	👍	☝	😐	✈	☠	46
→	😐	☹	✋	👉	❖	49
→	👎	🏴	💣	✋	☠	32
→	🏴	✈	⌘	☺	💣	45
→	⌘	☹	☺	❖	👉	68
39	33	70	39	54	44	67

😐	=	2
💣	=	3
👎	=	4
✈	=	5
✋	=	6
⌘	=	7
❖	=	8
🏴	=	9
☠	=	10
👍	=	11
👉	=	13
👆	=	14
☝	=	18
☹	=	19
☹	=	21

↘	↓	↓	↓	↓	↓	↙
→	11	18	2	5	10	46
→	2	19	6	14	8	49
→	4	9	3	6	10	32
→	9	5	7	21	3	45
→	7	19	21	8	13	68
39	33	70	39	54	44	67

© Les Page 2020   ISBN 9781913565084

PUZZLE 12

15 EMOJIS have different numerical values. Put the values in the puzzle grid to agree the sum totals horizontally, vertically and diagonally.

↓ = ∩ Enter values when worked out   Yellow boxes are "given" values

Cross out numerical values when placed

1 x	👈	=	
2 x	😐	=	19
1 x	👉	=	2
2 x	❖	=	
2 x	✈	=	
2 x	✋	=	15
2 x	☹	=	
2 x	☺	=	9
1 x	👍	=	14
2 x	💣	=	
2 x	⌘	=	
1 x	☝	=	5
2 x	🚩	=	
1 x	👎	=	8
2 x	☠	=	

X

Cross out list: 1, 2, 5, 6, 7, 8, 9, 11, 12, 14, 15, 17, 19, 20, 21

↘	↓	↓	↓	↓	↓	↙
→	💣	⌘	✋	👍	😐	86
→	☺	☝	💣	✋	☹	57
→	⌘	❖	👎	☠	☹	67
→	✈	☺	❖	😐	☠	61
→	🚩	🚩	👈	✈	👉	22
52	54	43	59	74	63	51

↘	↓	↓	↓	↓	↓	↙
→			15	14	19	86
→	9	5		15		57
→			8			67
→		9		19		61
→					2	22
52	54	43	59	74	63	51

Solution Overleaf

© Les Page 2020   ISBN 9781913565084   For more www.tarquingroup.com

SOLUTION 12

↘	↓	↓	↓	↓	↓	↙
→	💣	⌘	✋	👍	🙂	86
→	☺	☝	💣	✋	🙁	57
→	⌘	✦	👎	☠	🙁	67
→	✈	☺	✦	😐	☠	61
→	🚩	🚩	👈	✈	👉	22
52	54	43	59	74	63	51

🚩	=	1
👉	=	2
☝	=	5
✈	=	6
✦	=	7
👎	=	8
☺	=	9
🙁	=	11
👈	=	12
👍	=	14
✋	=	15
💣	=	17
😐	=	19
☠	=	20
⌘	=	21

↘	↓	↓	↓	↓	↓	↙
→	17	21	15	14	19	86
→	9	5	17	15	11	57
→	21	7	8	20	11	67
→	6	9	7	19	20	61
→	1	1	12	6	2	22
52	54	43	59	74	63	51

© Les Page 2020   ISBN 9781913565084

EMOJIS CHAIN REACTION

LEVEL **E**

PUZZLE 13

15 EMOJIS have different numerical values. Put the values in the puzzle grid to agree the sum totals horizontally, vertically and diagonally.

↓ = ↩ Enter values when worked out   Yellow boxes are "given" values

Cross out numerical values when placed

1 x	👈	=	5
2 x	😐	=	20
1 x	👉	=	
2 x	❖	=	
2 x	✈	=	7
2 x	✋	=	21
2 x	☹	=	
2 x	☺	=	
1 x	👍	=	
2 x	💣	=	
2 x	⌘	=	
1 x	☝	=	
2 x	🚩	=	10
1 x	👎	=	
2 x	☠	=	

↘	↓	↓	↓	↓	↓	↙
→	✋	👎	👍	☹	⌘	77
→	☺	👈	👉	✈	✈	46
→	💣	💣	😐	☹	☠	71
→	☺	🚩	😐	✋	⌘	84
→	❖	🚩	☝	❖	☠	25
53	70	54	59	61	59	78

↘	↓	↓	↓	↓	↓	↙
→	21					77
→		5		7	7	46
→			20			71
→			10	20	21	84
→		10				25
53	70	54	59	61	59	78

1
2
5
7
8
9
10
11
12
15
16
17
18
20
21

Solution Overleaf

© Les Page 2020   ISBN 9781913565084   For more www.tarquingroup.com

EMOJIS
CHAIN REACTION

LEVEL **E**

SOLUTION 13

↘	↓	↓	↓	↓	↓	↙
→	🖐	👎	👍	☹	⌘	77
→	☺	👈	👉	✈	✈	46
→	💣💥	💣	😐	☹	☠	71
→	☺	🚩	😐	🖐	⌘	84
→	✤	🚩	☝	✤	☠	25
53	70	54	59	61	59	78

✤	=	1
☝	=	2
👈	=	5
✈	=	7
👍	=	8
👉	=	9
🚩	=	10
☠	=	11
💣💥	=	12
⌘	=	15
☹	=	16
👎	=	17
☺	=	18
😐	=	20
🖐	=	21

↘	↓	↓	↓	↓	↓	↙
→	21	17	8	16	15	77
→	18	5	9	7	7	46
→	12	12	20	16	11	71
→	18	10	20	21	15	84
→	1	10	2	1	11	25
53	70	54	59	61	59	78

© Les Page 2020   ISBN 9781913565084

For more www.tarquingroup.com

EMOJIS CHAIN REACTION

PUZZLE 14

15 EMOJIS have different numerical values. Put the values in the puzzle grid to agree the sum totals horizontally, vertically and diagonally.

↓ = ∩ Enter values when worked out   Yellow boxes are "given" values

Cross out numerical values when placed

1 x	☞	=	9
2 x	😐	=	
1 x	☞	=	
2 x	❖	=	2
2 x	✈	=	14
2 x	✋	=	
2 x	☹	=	
2 x	☺	=	15
1 x	👍	=	
2 x	💣	=	
2 x	⌘	=	
1 x	☝	=	
2 x	⚑	=	21
1 x	👎	=	6
2 x	☠	=	20

↘	↓	↓	↓	↓	↓	↙
→	⌘	⌘	☹	✈	⚑	68
→	❖	❖	😐	☠	✋	40
→	☺	💣	✈	☞	☹	57
→	💣	☺	☝	👎	👍	49
→	⚑	✋	😐	☠	☞	66
91	73	55	46	68	38	47

↘	↓	↓	↓	↓	↓	↙
→				14	21	68
→	2	2		20		40
→	15		14			57
→		15		6		49
→	21			20	9	66
91	73	55	46	68	38	47

1
2
3
4
5
6
8
9
13
14
15
16
19
20
21

Solution Overleaf

© Les Page 2020   ISBN 9781913565084   For more www.tarquingroup.com

EMOJIS CHAIN REACTION

SOLUTION 14

↘	↓	↓	↓	↓	↓	↙
→	⌘	⌘	☹	✈	🏳	68
→	❖	❖	😐	☠	✋	40
→	☺	💣	✈	☞	☹	57
→	💣	☺	☝	👎	👍	49
→	🏳	✋	😐	☠	☜	66
91	73	55	46	68	38	47

☹	=	1
❖	=	2
✋	=	3
👍	=	4
☝	=	5
👎	=	6
☞	=	8
☜	=	9
😐	=	13
✈	=	14
☺	=	15
⌘	=	16
💣	=	19
☠	=	20
🏳	=	21

↘	↓	↓	↓	↓	↓	↙
→	16	16	1	14	21	68
→	2	2	13	20	3	40
→	15	19	14	8	1	57
→	19	15	5	6	4	49
→	21	3	13	20	9	66
91	73	55	46	68	38	47

© Les Page 2020   ISBN 9781913565084

PUZZLE 15

15 EMOJIS have different numerical values. Put the values in the puzzle grid to agree the sum totals horizontally, vertically and diagonally.

↓ = ⤴ Enter values when worked out   Yellow boxes are "given" values

Cross out numerical values when placed ✖

1 x	👉	=	3
2 x	😐	=	6
1 x	👉	=	1
2 x	❖	=	
2 x	✈	=	2
2 x	🖐	=	
2 x	☹	=	
2 x	☺	=	5
1 x	👍	=	7
2 x	💣	=	
2 x	⌘	=	8
1 x	☝	=	
2 x	🏳	=	
1 x	👎	=	
2 x	☠	=	21

↘	↓	↓	↓	↓	↓	↙
→	❖	✈	☹	💣	☝	52
→	☹	⌘	☺	✈	💣	42
→	👎	⌘	👉	🖐	🏳	55
→	☠	☺	☠	😐	🖐	72
→	❖	😐	🏳	👉	👍	36
33	78	29	53	40	57	37

↘	↓	↓	↓	↓	↓	↙
→		2				52
→		8	5	2		42
→		8	3			55
→	21	5	21	6		72
→		6		1	7	36
33	78	29	53	40	57	37

Cross-out values: 1, 2, 3, 5, 6, 7, 8, 9, 10, 12, 13, 15, 16, 19, 21

Solution Overleaf

© Les Page 2020   ISBN 9781913565084   For more www.tarquingroup.com

SOLUTION 15

↘	↓	↓	↓	↓	↓	↙
→	❖	✈	☹	💣	☝	52
→	☹	⌘	☺	✈	💣	42
→	👎	⌘	👉	✋	🚩	55
→	☠	☺	☠	😐	✋	72
→	❖	😐	🚩	☞	👍	36
33	78	29	53	40	57	37

↘	↓	↓	↓	↓	↓	↙
→	13	2	15	12	10	52
→	15	8	5	2	12	42
→	16	8	3	19	9	55
→	21	5	21	6	19	72
→	13	6	9	1	7	36
33	78	29	53	40	57	37

☞	=	1
✈	=	2
👉	=	3
☺	=	5
😐	=	6
👍	=	7
⌘	=	8
🚩	=	9
☝	=	10
💣	=	12
❖	=	13
☹	=	15
👎	=	16
✋	=	19
☠	=	21

© Les Page 2020   ISBN 9781913565084

EMOJIS CHAIN REACTION

LEVEL **E**

PUZZLE 16

15 EMOJIS have different numerical values. Put the values in the puzzle grid to agree the sum totals horizontally, vertically and diagonally.

↓ = ↺ Enter values when worked out   Yellow boxes are "given" values

Cross out numerical values when placed

✗

1 x	🖘	=	
2 x	😐	=	3
1 x	👉	=	8
2 x	❖	=	
2 x	✈	=	18
2 x	✋	=	12
2 x	☹	=	
2 x	☺	=	
1 x	👍	=	1
2 x	💣	=	
2 x	⌘	=	11
1 x	☝	=	
2 x	🏳	=	
1 x	👎	=	14
2 x	☠	=	

↘	↓	↓	↓	↓	↓	↙
→	☹	😐	☺	👍	☠	33
→	👉	😐	❖	⌘	🏳	31
→	☠	☹	👎	☝	💣	49
→	❖	✋	👈	✈	🏳	49
→	💣	✈	✋	⌘	☺	56
46	30	45	53	58	32	57

↘	↓	↓	↓	↓	↓	↙
→		3		1		33
→	8	3		11		31
→			14			49
→		12		18		49
→		18	12	11		56
46	30	45	53	58	32	57

Number column (cross out):

| 1 |
| 2 |
| 3 |
| 4 |
| 5 |
| 7 |
| 8 |
| 9 |
| 10 |
| 11 |
| 12 |
| 13 |
| 14 |
| 17 |
| 18 |

Solution Overleaf

© Les Page 2020   ISBN 9781913565084   For more www.tarquingroup.com

SOLUTION 16

↘	↓	↓	↓	↓	↓	↙
→	☹	😐	☺	👍	☠	33
→	☞	😐	❖	⌘	⚑	31
→	☠	☹	👎	☝	💣	49
→	❖	✋	👉	✈	⚑	49
→	💣	✈	✋	⌘	☺	56
46	30	45	53	58	32	57

👍	=	1
💣	=	2
😐	=	3
❖	=	4
⚑	=	5
☠	=	7
☞	=	8
☹	=	9
👉	=	10
⌘	=	11
✋	=	12
☺	=	13
👎	=	14
☝	=	17
✈	=	18

↘	↓	↓	↓	↓	↓	↙
→	9	3	13	1	7	33
→	8	3	4	11	5	31
→	7	9	14	17	2	49
→	4	12	10	18	5	49
→	2	18	12	11	13	56
46	30	45	53	58	32	57

© Les Page 2020   ISBN 9781913565084

EMOJIS CHAIN REACTION

PUZZLE 17

15 EMOJIS have different numerical values. Put the values in the puzzle grid to agree the sum totals horizontally, vertically and diagonally.

↓ = ∩ Enter values when worked out   Yellow boxes are "given" values

Cross out numerical values when placed ✗

1 x	👉	=	
2 x	😐	=	
1 x	👉	=	6
2 x	❖	=	7
2 x	✈	=	
2 x	✋	=	
2 x	☹	=	11
2 x	☺	=	20
1 x	👍	=	15
2 x	💣	=	
2 x	⌘	=	2
1 x	☝	=	5
2 x	🏳	=	
1 x	👎	=	
2 x	☠	=	

↘	↓	↓	↓	↓	↓	↙
→	😐	✈	⌘	✋	🏳	44
→	👉	⌘	✋	☝	✈	42
→	💣	☹	☹	😐	👉	54
→	🏳	☺	☺	❖	👎	64
→	☠	❖	💣	☠	👍	69
58	47	57	54	53	62	45

↘	↓	↓	↓	↓	↓	↙
→			2			44
→	6	2		5		42
→		11	11			54
→		20	20	7		64
→		7			15	69
58	47	57	54	53	62	45

2
3
5
6
7
9
10
11
12
13
14
15
17
19
20

Solution Overleaf

© Les Page 2020   ISBN 9781913565084   For more www.tarquingroup.com

EMOJIS CHAIN REACTION

LEVEL E

SOLUTION 17

↘	↓	↓	↓	↓	↓	↙
→	😐	✈	⌘	✋	🏳	44
→	👉	⌘	✋	☝	✈	42
→	💣	☹	☹	😐	👉	54
→	🏳	☺	☺	✦	👎	64
→	☠	✦	💣	☠	👍	69
58	47	57	54	53	62	45

⌘	=	2
🏳	=	3
☝	=	5
👉	=	6
✦	=	7
💣	=	9
😐	=	10
☹	=	11
✋	=	12
👉	=	13
👎	=	14
👍	=	15
✈	=	17
☠	=	19
☺	=	20

↘	↓	↓	↓	↓	↓	↙
→	10	17	2	12	3	44
→	6	2	12	5	17	42
→	9	11	11	10	13	54
→	3	20	20	7	14	64
→	19	7	9	19	15	69
58	47	57	54	53	62	45

© Les Page 2020   ISBN 9781913565084

For more www.tarquingroup.com

PUZZLE 18

15 EMOJIS have different numerical values. Put the values in the puzzle grid to agree the sum totals horizontally, vertically and diagonally.

↓ = ∩ Enter values when worked out   Yellow boxes are "given" values

 Cross out numerical values when placed

N x	Emoji	=	Value
1 x	👈	=	7
2 x	😐	=	6
1 x	👉	=	10
2 x	✣	=	12
2 x	✈	=	
2 x	🖐	=	16
2 x	☹	=	
2 x	😊	=	
1 x	👍	=	
2 x	💣	=	
2 x	⌘	=	
1 x	☝	=	
2 x	🏳	=	17
1 x	👎	=	15
2 x	☠	=	

↘	↓	↓	↓	↓	↓	↙
→	👉	😊	😐	🖐	🏳	50
→	💣	👈	⌘	🖐	😊	47
→	⌘	☹	🏳	☹	☝	60
→	👍	✣	✈	👎	✈	73
→	✣	😐	☠	💣	☠	56
74	65	30	75	53	63	67

↘	↓	↓	↓	↓	↓	↙
→	10		6	16	17	50
→		7		16		47
→			17			60
→		12		15		73
→	12	6				56
74	65	30	75	53	63	67

Cross out
1
2
4
6
7
10
12
13
14
15
16
17
18
20
21

Solution Overleaf

© Les Page 2020   ISBN 9781913565084

For more www.tarquingroup.com

EMOJIS CHAIN REACTION

LEVEL **E**

SOLUTION 18

↘	↓	↓	↓	↓	↓	↙
→	☞	☺	☺	✋	⚑	50
→	💣	☞	⌘	✋	☺	47
→	⌘	☹	⚑	☹	☝	60
→	👍	❖	✈	👎	✈	73
→	❖	☺	☠	💣	☠	56
74	65	30	75	53	63	67

☺	=	1
💣	=	2
☹	=	4
☺	=	6
☞	=	7
☞	=	10
❖	=	12
✈	=	13
☝	=	14
👎	=	15
✋	=	16
⚑	=	17
☠	=	18
👍	=	20
⌘	=	21

↘	↓	↓	↓	↓	↓	↙
→	10	1	6	16	17	50
→	2	7	21	16	1	47
→	21	4	17	4	14	60
→	20	12	13	15	13	73
→	12	6	18	2	18	56
74	65	30	75	53	63	67

© Les Page 2020 ISBN 9781913565084

For more www.tarquingroup.com

EMOJIS CHAIN REACTION

PUZZLE 19

15 EMOJIS have different numerical values. Put the values in the puzzle grid to agree the sum totals horizontally, vertically and diagonally.

Cross out numerical values when placed

↓   =   ∩   Enter values when worked out   Yellow boxes are "given" values

		=	
1 x	👆	=	
2 x	😐	=	
1 x	👉	=	
2 x	❖	=	17
2 x	✈	=	
2 x	🖐	=	
2 x	☹	=	15
2 x	☺	=	
1 x	👍	=	10
2 x	💣	=	19
2 x	⌘	=	
1 x	☝	=	
2 x	🚩	=	21
1 x	👎	=	16
2 x	☠	=	

↘	↓	↓	↓	↓	↓	↙
→	🖐	✈	👆	🖐	☹	67
→	🚩	🚩	☠	👎	👉	69
→	👍	☺	☹	❖	☠	64
→	😐	💣	😐	❖	✈	58
→	⌘	☺	💣	☝	⌘	76
85	73	72	69	68	52	87

↘	↓	↓	↓	↓	↓	↙
→					15	67
→	21	21		16		69
→	10		15	17		64
→		19		17		58
→			19			76
85	73	72	69	68	52	87

2
4
6
8
9
10
13
14
15
16
17
18
19
20
21

Solution Overleaf

© Les Page 2020   ISBN 9781913565084   For more www.tarquingroup.com

EMOJIS
CHAIN REACTION

SOLUTION 19

↘	↓	↓	↓	↓	↓	↙
→	🖐	✈	☞	🖐	☹	67
→	🏳	🏳	☠	👎	☞	69
→	👍	☺	☹	❖	☠	64
→	😐	💣	😐	❖	✈	58
→	⌘	☺	💣	☝	⌘	76
85	73	72	69	68	52	87

☞	=	2
☝	=	4
✈	=	6
😐	=	8
☠	=	9
👍	=	10
☺	=	13
🖐	=	14
☹	=	15
👎	=	16
❖	=	17
☞	=	18
💣	=	19
⌘	=	20
🏳	=	21

↘	↓	↓	↓	↓	↓	↙
→	14	6	18	14	15	67
→	21	21	9	16	2	69
→	10	13	15	17	9	64
→	8	19	8	17	6	58
→	20	13	19	4	20	76
85	73	72	69	68	52	87

© Les Page 2020   ISBN 9781913565084

EMOJIS CHAIN REACTION

LEVEL **E**

PUZZLE 20

15 EMOJIS have different numerical values. Put the values in the puzzle grid to agree the sum totals horizontally, vertically and diagonally.

Cross out numerical values when placed

	↓	=	⌒ Enter values when worked out		Yellow boxes are "given" values

1 x	👉	=	7
2 x	😐	=	8
1 x	👉	=	
2 x	✦	=	
2 x	✈	=	
2 x	🖐	=	12
2 x	☹	=	4
2 x	☺	=	14
1 x	👍	=	
2 x	💣	=	
2 x	⌘	=	
1 x	☝	=	
2 x	🏳	=	
1 x	👎	=	
2 x	☠	=	15

↘	↓	↓	↓	↓	↓	↙
→	☝	🖐	☠	👉	✦	57
→	🏳	☠	☹	👉	☹	40
→	✈	💣	😐	☺	⌘	71
→	👎	🖐	✈	☺	🏳	74
→	😐	👍	⌘	💣	✦	49
44	58	58	60	70	45	48

↘	↓	↓	↓	↓	↓	↙
→		12	15			57
→		15	4	7	4	40
→			8	14		71
→		12		14		74
→	8					49
44	58	58	60	70	45	48

2	3
4	7
8	9
10	12
13	14
15	16
18	19
20	

Solution Overleaf

© Les Page 2020   ISBN 9781913565084

For more www.tarquingroup.com

EMOJIS CHAIN REACTION

SOLUTION 20

↘	↓	↓	↓	↓	↓	↙
→	☝	✋	☠	☞	❖	57
→	⚐	☠	☹	☞	☹	40
→	✈	💣	😐	☺	⌘	71
→	👎	✋	✈	☺	⚐	74
→	😐	👍	⌘	💣	❖	49
44	58	58	60	70	45	48

☝	=	2
👍	=	3
☹	=	4
☞	=	7
😐	=	8
❖	=	9
⚐	=	10
✋	=	12
⌘	=	13
☺	=	14
☠	=	15
💣	=	16
👎	=	18
☞	=	19
✈	=	20

↘	↓	↓	↓	↓	↓	↙
→	2	12	15	19	9	57
→	10	15	4	7	4	40
→	20	16	8	14	13	71
→	18	12	20	14	10	74
→	8	3	13	16	9	49
44	58	58	60	70	45	48

© Les Page 2020   ISBN 9781913565084

For more www.tarquingroup.com

EMOJIS CHAIN REACTION

PUZZLE 21

15 EMOJIS have different numerical values. Put the values in the puzzle grid to agree the sum totals horizontally, vertically and diagonally.

↓ = ∩ Enter values when worked out   Yellow boxes are "given" values

Cross out numerical values when placed

Count	Emoji	=	Value
1 x	🖐	=	17
2 x	🙂	=	9
1 x	👉	=	6
2 x	❖	=	20
2 x	✈	=	
2 x	✋	=	
2 x	☹	=	
2 x	☺	=	
1 x	👍	=	8
2 x	💣	=	
2 x	⌘	=	10
1 x	☝	=	7
2 x	🚩	=	
1 x	👎	=	12
2 x	☠	=	

Crossed-out numerical values column: 2, 3, 6, 7, 8, 9, 10, 12, 13, 15, 16, 17, 18, 19, 20

Top grid

↘	↓	↓	↓	↓	↓	↙	
→	☹	👉(pointing)	✋	✋	☠	78	
→	🙂	👉	✈	👎	💣	44	
→	✈	☺	👍	💣	🚩	46	
→	🚩	⌘	☺	❖	❖	71	
→	☝	☠	⌘	☹	🙂	61	
56	37	70	51	76	66	59	

Bottom grid (values)

↘	↓	↓	↓	↓	↓	↙
→		17				78
→	9	6		12		44
→			8			46
→		10		20	20	71
→	7		10		9	61
56	37	70	51	76	66	59

Solution Overleaf

© Les Page 2020   ISBN 9781913565084

SOLUTION 21

↘	↓	↓	↓	↓	↓	↙
→	☹	☜	✋	✋	☠	78
→	😐	☞	✈	👎	💣	44
→	✈	☺	👍	💣	🏳	46
→	🏳	⌘	☺	❖	❖	71
→	☝	☠	⌘	☹	😐	61
56	37	70	51	76	66	59

↘	↓	↓	↓	↓	↓	↙
→	16	17	13	13	19	78
→	9	6	2	12	15	44
→	2	18	8	15	3	46
→	3	10	18	20	20	71
→	7	19	10	16	9	61
56	37	70	51	76	66	59

✈	=	2
🏳	=	3
☞	=	6
☝	=	7
👍	=	8
😐	=	9
⌘	=	10
👎	=	12
✋	=	13
💣	=	15
☹	=	16
☜	=	17
☺	=	18
☠	=	19
❖	=	20

© Les Page 2020   ISBN 9781913565084

For more www.tarquingroup.com

PUZZLE 22

15 EMOJIS have different numerical values. Put the values in the puzzle grid to agree the sum totals horizontally, vertically and diagonally.

Cross out numerical values when placed

✗

↓ = ∩ Enter values when worked out   Yellow boxes are "given" values

1 x	👉	=	13
2 x	😐	=	
1 x	👉	=	
2 x	❖	=	
2 x	✈	=	
2 x	🖐	=	
2 x	☹	=	
2 x	☺	=	
1 x	👍	=	11
2 x	💣	=	14
2 x	⌘	=	12
1 x	☝	=	
2 x	🏳	=	17
1 x	👎	=	15
2 x	☠	=	3

↘	↓	↓	↓	↓	↓	↙
→	☠	❖	😐	🖐	☹	50
→	🖐	👉	☹	👎	☝	60
→	✈	☺	💣	⌘	🏳	51
→	✈	🏳	☺	⌘	❖	45
→	👍	💣	☠	👉	😐	65
61	45	54	39	79	54	58

2	
3	
4	
6	
8	
9	
11	
12	
13	
14	
15	
16	
17	
19	
21	

↘	↓	↓	↓	↓	↓	↙
→	3					50
→		13		15		60
→			14	12	17	51
→		17		12		45
→	11	14	3			65
61	45	54	39	79	54	58

Solution Overleaf

© Les Page 2020   ISBN 9781913565084   For more www.tarquingroup.com

EMOJIS
CHAIN REACTION

SOLUTION 22

↘	↓	↓	↓	↓	↓	↙
→	☠	❖	☺	✋	☹	50
→	✋	☞	☹	👎	☝	60
→	✈	☺	💣	⌘	⚑	51
→	✈	⚑	☺	⌘	❖	45
→	👍	💣	☠	☞	☺	65
61	45	54	39	79	54	58

☺	=	2
☠	=	3
☹	=	4
✈	=	6
❖	=	8
☝	=	9
👍	=	11
⌘	=	12
☞	=	13
💣	=	14
👎	=	15
☺	=	16
⚑	=	17
✋	=	19
☞	=	21

↘	↓	↓	↓	↓	↓	↙
→	3	8	16	19	4	50
→	19	13	4	15	9	60
→	6	2	14	12	17	51
→	6	17	2	12	8	45
→	11	14	3	21	16	65
61	45	54	39	79	54	58

© Les Page 2020   ISBN 9781913565084

For more www.tarquingroup.com

EMOJIS CHAIN REACTION

Cross out numerical values when placed

PUZZLE 23

15 EMOJIS have different numerical values. Put the values in the puzzle grid to agree the sum totals horizontally, vertically and diagonally.

↓ = ∩ Enter values when worked out   Yellow boxes are "given" values

1 x	👆	=	
2 x	😐	=	19
1 x	👉	=	
2 x	❖	=	
2 x	✈	=	
2 x	🖐	=	
2 x	☹	=	
2 x	☺	=	7
1 x	👍	=	
2 x	💣	=	16
2 x	⌘	=	
1 x	☝	=	6
2 x	🚩	=	8
1 x	👎	=	
2 x	☠	=	17

↘	↓	↓	↓	↓	↓	↙
→	😐	👆	✈	🖐	☹	66
→	👉	💣	☠	😐	❖	74
→	⌘	✈	☠	☺	👆	41
→	👍	☺	❖	🚩	⌘	22
→	👎	☹	💣	🚩	🖐	58
63	53	56	62	56	34	74

↘	↓	↓	↓	↓	↓	↙
→	19					66
→	20	16	17	19		74
→			17	7	6	41
→		7		8		22
→			16	8		58
63	53	56	62	56	34	74

1
2
4
6
7
8
9
10
11
12
14
16
17
19
20

Solution Overleaf

© Les Page 2020   ISBN 9781913565084   For more www.tarquingroup.com

EMOJIS CHAIN REACTION

SOLUTION 23

↘	↓	↓	↓	↓	↓	↙
→	😐	☞	✈	✋	☹	66
→	☞	💣	☠	😐	❖	74
→	⌘	✈	☠	☺	☝	41
→	👍	☺	❖	🚩	⌘	22
→	👎	☹	💣	🚩	✋	58
63	53	56	62	56	34	74

⌘	=	1
❖	=	2
👍	=	4
☝	=	6
☺	=	7
🚩	=	8
👎	=	9
✈	=	10
☹	=	11
☞	=	12
✋	=	14
💣	=	16
☠	=	17
😐	=	19
☞	=	20

↘	↓	↓	↓	↓	↓	↙
→	19	12	10	14	11	66
→	20	16	17	19	2	74
→	1	10	17	7	6	41
→	4	7	2	8	1	22
→	9	11	16	8	14	58
63	53	56	62	56	34	74

© Les Page 2020   ISBN 9781913565084   For more www.tarquingroup.com

EMOJIS CHAIN REACTION

LEVEL **E**

PUZZLE 24

15 EMOJIS have different numerical values. Put the values in the puzzle grid to agree the sum totals horizontally, vertically and diagonally.

Cross out numerical values when placed

↓ = ↻ Enter values when worked out   Yellow boxes are "given" values

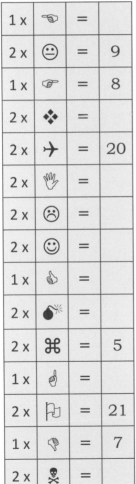

1 x	👆	=	
2 x	😐	=	9
1 x	👉	=	8
2 x	❖	=	
2 x	✈	=	20
2 x	✋	=	
2 x	☹	=	
2 x	☺	=	
1 x	👍	=	
2 x	💣	=	
2 x	⌘	=	5
1 x	👆	=	
2 x	🏳	=	21
1 x	👎	=	7
2 x	☠	=	

↘	↓	↓	↓	↓	↓	↙
→	☠	✋	👍	👎	💣	53
→	💣	👉	☠	🏳	❖	66
→	☹	☹	⌘	✈	☺	57
→	❖	✈	☺	😐	👆	67
→	⌘	😐	👆	✋	🏳	49
66	55	61	34	68	74	47

↘	↓	↓	↓	↓	↓	↙
→				7		53
→		8		21		66
→			5	20		57
→		20		9		67
→	5	9			21	49
66	55	61	34	68	74	47

3
4
5
6
7
8
9
11
13
14
15
16
18
20
21

Solution Overleaf

© Les Page 2020   ISBN 9781913565084
For more www.tarquingroup.com

EMOJIS
CHAIN REACTION

LEVEL E

SOLUTION 24

↘	↓	↓	↓	↓	↓	↙
→	☠	✋	👍	👎	💣	53
→	💣	☞	☠	🏳	❖	66
→	☹	☹	⌘	✈	☺	57
→	❖	✈	☺	😐	☞	67
→	⌘	😐	☝	✋	🏳	49
66	55	61	34	68	74	47

☝	=	3
☠	=	4
⌘	=	5
☺	=	6
👎	=	7
☞	=	8
😐	=	9
✋	=	11
☹	=	13
👉	=	14
💣	=	15
👍	=	16
❖	=	18
✈	=	20
🏳	=	21

↘	↓	↓	↓	↓	↓	↙
→	4	11	16	7	15	53
→	15	8	4	21	18	66
→	13	13	5	20	6	57
→	18	20	6	9	14	67
→	5	9	3	11	21	49
66	55	61	34	68	74	47

© Les Page 2020   ISBN 9781913565084

PUZZLE

AT FIRST GLANCE IT MAY LOOK IMPOSSIBLE TO DO! ☹
BUT USING YOUR INITIATIVE IT CAN BE DONE! NEVER GIVE UP. ✍

PLACE THESE 33 NUMBERS CORRECTLY TO SOLVE THIS PUZZLE

3	4	8	13	14	16	16	17	17	17	19
21	21	22	25	27	31	33	34	35	36	38
38	47	49	50	53	54	59	92	94	125	141

Just plus... that's all you've got to do!

9	+	☐	=	☐	+	☐	=	☐	+	16	=	☐
+		+		+		+		+		+		+
12	+	5	=	☐	+	☐	=	☐	+	☐	=	☐
=		=		=		=		=		=		=
21	+	13	=	☐	+	☐	=	☐	+	☐	=	☐
+		+		+		+		+		+		+
13	+	☐	=	☐	+	☐	=	☐	+	☐	=	☐
=		=		=		=		=		=		=
34	+	☐	=	☐	+	44	=	☐	+	☐	=	☐
+		+		+		+		+		+		+
2	+	11	=	☐	+	18	=	☐	+	☐	=	☐
=		=		=		=		=		=		=
☐	+	☐	=	63	+	62	=	☐	+	69	=	194

Solution Overleaf

© Les Page 2020   ISBN 9781913565084

For more www.tarquingroup.com

SOLUTION

INITATIVE USED.

IT CAN BE DONE !

👌

☺

EVERYTHING ADDED = THE TOTALS !

9	+	8	=	17	+	21	=	38	+	16	=	54
+		+		+		+		+		+		+
12	+	5	=	17	+	4	=	21	+	17	=	38
=		=		=		=		=		=		=
21	+	13	=	34	+	25	=	59	+	33	=	92
+		+		+		+		+		+		+
13	+	3	=	16	+	19	=	35	+	14	=	49
=		=		=		=		=		=		=
34	+	16	=	50	+	44	=	94	+	47	=	141
+		+		+		+		+		+		+
2	+	11	=	13	+	18	=	31	+	22	=	53
=		=		=		=		=		=		=
36	+	27	=	63	+	62	=	125	+	69	=	194

© Les Page 2020   ISBN 9781913565084

For more www.tarquingroup.com

PUZZLE

USE YOUR " GREY MATTER " TO SOLVE THIS PUZZLE !

?	A	B	?
THIS	×	+	TOTAL
12			115
11			19
10			71
9			83
8			42
7			93
6			38
5			18
4			13
3			21
2			34
1			14

A	B
×	+
1	1
2	2
3	3
4	4
5	5
6	6
7	7
8	8
9	9
10	10
11	11
12	12

Numbers in A & B can only be used once.

Cross off numbers in A & B once placed. Not sure? See the example below!

DO NOT

JUMP TO ☠

CONCLUSIONS!

☹

YOU HAVE

BEEN WARNED !

Example:

THIS	×	A	+	B	=	TOTAL
12	×	2	+	1	=	25

In the example you would cross off 2 in A & 1 in B.

Solution Overleaf

© Les Page 2020   ISBN 9781913565084   For more www.tarquingroup.com

SOLUTION

👆 GOT IT RIGHT !

☺	A	B	=
THIS	X	+	TOTAL
12	9	7	115
11	1	8	19
10	7	1	71
9	8	11	83
8	4	10	42
7	12	9	93
6	6	2	38
5	3	3	18
4	2	5	13
3	5	6	21
2	11	12	34
1	10	4	14

© Les Page 2020   ISBN 9781913565084   For more www.tarquingroup.com

PUZZLE PREVIEW
THE WAREHOUSE

PUZZLE

WHAT'S IN STORE HERE ?

A warehouse has 25 large rooms. Each room has six storage areas numbered from 1 to 6. Each room has interlinking glass doors to other rooms. The storage areas adjacent to the interlinking glass doors have the same storage area number as shown in the example below:

6 / 6 or 4 | 4

↖ ↗ interlinking glass doors

Insert the missing storage area numbers so that each room contains storage area numbers 1 to 6.

3	5	1
1	5	2
4	3	6
5	3	2

			1		4			
3	4	5		3		2		6
		6				1		4
6								3
4			3		6			4
1								5
6		4				3		4
5								1
2		1				4		3
3								6
1			2			5		4
2			3					2
5		4			6			5
6								6
4			5		4			1
5				3				5
	3		4			1	3	
			6	5				

Solution Overleaf

© Les Page 2020 ISBN 9781913565084

For more www.tarquingroup.com

SOLUTION

LOOK ! ↘ HAVING "DONE TIME" PROVES IT CAN BE SOLVED !   ◐   ☺

			1	6	4			
3	4	5	5	3	2	2	3	6
2	1	6	6	3	1	1	5	4
6	1	5	5	4	2	2	5	3
4	2	3	3	4	6	6	1	4
1	2	5	5	1	2	2	1	5
6	3	4	4	1	3	3	6	4
5	3	6	6	2	5	5	6	1
2	4	1	1	2	4	4	2	3
3	4	5	5	6	3	3	2	6
1	6	2	2	6	5	5	1	4
2	6	3	3	1	4	4	1	2
5	1	4	4	1	6	6	3	5
6	1	3	3	2	5	5	3	6
4	2	5	5	2	4	4	2	1
5	2	1	1	3	6	6	2	5
6	3	4	4	3	1	1	3	4
			6	5	2			

© Les Page 2020   ISBN 9781913565084

For more www.tarquingroup.com

PUZZLE

YOU WILL NEVER ESCAPE " DOING TIME " ON THIS PUZZLE !

Every block MUST contain 1, 2, 3 & 4 in the left hand column and 1 to 32 MUST be placed in the centre columns to agree the totals.

Cross out numerical values when placed

1	2	3
4	5	6
7	8	9
10	11	12
13	14	15
16	17	18
19	20	21
22	23	24
25	26	27
28	29	30
31	32	☺

Block 1

1	+		=	11
	+		=	17
	+		=	26
4	+		=	16

Block 2

3	+		=	8
	+		=	36
	+		=	7
	+		=	32

Block 3

3	+		=	14
	+		=	28
	+		=	30
	+		=	22

Block 4

1	+		=	2
	+		=	19
	+		=	29
2	+		=	23

Block 5

3	+		=	22
	+		=	15
4	+		=	27
	+		=	4

Block 6

4	+		=	24
	+		=	4
	+		=	27
	+		=	20

Block 7

1	+		=	16
	+		=	9
	+		=	32
	+		=	13

Block 8

4	+		=	8
	+		=	9
2	+		=	33
	+		=	25

Solution Overleaf

© Les Page 2020   ISBN 9781913565084

SOLUTION

LOOK ! ↘ HAVING "DONE TIME" PROVES IT CAN BE SOLVED ! ✋ ☺

1	+	10	=	11
3	+	14	=	17
2	+	24	=	26
4	+	12	=	16

3	+	5	=	8
4	+	32	=	36
1	+	6	=	7
2	+	30	=	32

3	+	11	=	14
1	+	27	=	28
2	+	28	=	30
4	+	18	=	22

1	+	1	=	2
3	+	16	=	19
4	+	25	=	29
2	+	21	=	23

3	+	19	=	22
2	+	13	=	15
4	+	23	=	27
1	+	3	=	4

4	+	20	=	24
2	+	2	=	4
1	+	26	=	27
3	+	17	=	20

1	+	15	=	16
2	+	7	=	9
3	+	29	=	32
4	+	9	=	13

4	+	4	=	8
1	+	8	=	9
2	+	31	=	33
3	+	22	=	25

© Les Page 2020   ISBN 9781913565084

Scribble Page

Need a New Tarquin Challenge?

We have a series of number and logic puzzles for a variety of ages and skill levels. See all at our website - but here are a selection:

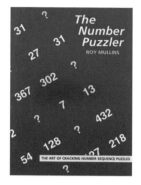
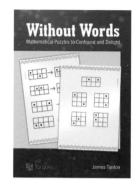
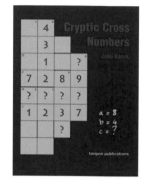

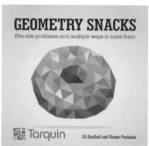

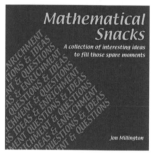

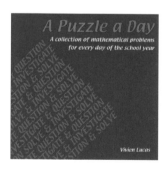
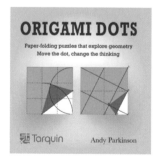

Bestselling titles like Without Words, Geometry Snacks and A Puzzle a Day will be joined by Birds, Bees and Burgers in 2021.

Buy Tarquin books in most trade outlets or from www.tarquingroup.com